Bootcamp For Business

Russell Payne

Copyright Russell Payne 2016

IBSN 978-0-9934546-3-9

Published by FCM PUBLISHING

www.fcmpublishing.co.uk

Contents

For Katie, my life's love,
Eleanor, my princess, and
Henry, my favourite (and only)
son.

" thank you for the Business Bootcamp. I enjoyed every minute, some top tips. I served for 16 years in the military, 4 of which was with Special operations. For the past two years I have suffered with PTSD from Afghanistan, I lost my family, friends and all confidence. I have to say that, after the Bootcamp which was delivered with such passion and enthusiasm, I feel inspired to achieve success. Its been a long time since I could genuinely say I'm excited about my future, I'm so grateful for the wake up call. "

Steve Cottam FFA LTD

Foreword

Anyone who knows Russell, would confirm that he lives his brand. The ever changing and eye catching signs outside his offices or the livery on his vehicles confirm he does things differently. His Bootcamps and 777 events are fun, engaging and packed with great ideas and simple message.

I was therefore interested to read his book and as I hoped, it records these tips and anecdotes in a simple way, that leaves you thinking about how you could apply them in your own business or to the way you think.

This is an easy read that you can pick up, put down and return to. It is the sort of book that you could keep in your briefcase and read again when you want to refocus on your business.

At first I thought that the book was aimed at the small and medium sized business community but as I read on, I realised that the points he makes apply to businesses of any size.

Having an accountancy practice leading the way in being different is very different indeed!

Paul Barron CBE
Management Consultant Human Alchemy
(Former CEO of NATS, UK President of Alstom, CEO of Alstom Gas Turbines)

Introduction

Everybody wants to grow their business. It's simple. Sit in front of your computer, go online, type in 'business growth books' and take your pick from literally thousands of different titles. In the main, they're all good books built around ideas of goal setting, business plans and self-development. If you're anything like me, you'll have a whole collection of these books, usually bought at the airport before flying off on holiday. I read them on the two-hour flight to Spain and highlight the best bits for future use. Of course, this will result in dramatic and immediate action as soon as I'm back. Er...

In fact, what usually happens is that the latest book joins the others already on my office bookshelf. The quiet day when I have time to read them again never comes and, rather than making great strides in self-development, all I've achieved is 'shelf development'.

These are good books, so why isn't everyone already successfully growing their business? Maybe it's because that times have changed and the world moves so quickly today that successful marketing changes month by month, rather than year on year. So this book is a collection of my thoughts on the need for early adoption of technologies, personalisation and originality in marketing. It's all about your business, your originality, your individual application of classic solutions. It's also about how my highly successful Business Bootcamps came into being.

Some years ago, a good friend of mine, David Gill, the managing director of Peak Performance, asked me to put together a workshop containing as many ideas as possible to help business owners grow their businesses. In a very rough and ready fashion, I put together what was to become the basis of the first Business Bootcamp. At that time, it was really just a collection of tips and strategies from all the great motivational videos I had seen over the years, plus a few of my own ideas thrown in. In the end, that workshop never happened, but the idea stayed in my mind.

Some time later, I picked up the idea again and started to work on it in earnest for myself. Business Bootcamp was born and it has evolved over the years into a highly popular and successful marketing event that works for me as well as the businesses that attend. It's about brainstorming ideas that work, identifying those that don't, the importance of doing things differently and how to stand out from the crowd.

Now, if your reaction is 'this is all just common sense', I couldn't agree more. But though it's called common sense, it really isn't that common at all. That's why my Business Bootcamp events continue to be relevant.

Growing a business is not rocket science: it's a step-by-step process of applying systems and marketing ideas that work when systematically applied. Some of the ideas will be relevant to your business and some will not, but they do all work when done well.

I hope after you've read the book you'll be inspired to try some of these ideas and will gain real value from them. I can assure you that very few of the ideas in the book are entirely of my own invention and I make no apology for that. What I offer is the experience gained from working with hundreds of businesses to develop systems and marketing ideas that have worked for them. And, if them, why not you?

I wish you every success in growing your business.

Russell

ASK AN EXPERT

Throughout the book you will see several 'expert inserts'. This is where I have taken the opportunity to invite someone who I deem an expert in their field to provide a précis of what they do and how they do it. The fact that they are included in the book is a testimony that they have brought great value to my accountancy practice and me in a strategic alliance over the years. I hope you enjoy their case studies.

Certainly, I have found them invaluable.

NO SECOND CHANCE

Self-help and business development books all mention the importance of first impressions. The importance of the first 20 seconds... you don't get a second chance... first point of contact... blah, blah, blah.

Of course, it's true about first impressions with some clients, but not every client. Some points of contact may be so infrequent with certain clients that you have multiple opportunities to make a 'first' impression - maybe even every time you meet. Think about when you attend a business event and have time to meet and make new contacts. You may meet the same people several times before they need your service or product and start to look at you in a new light.

That's why you should never take your foot off the pedal. Take every opportunity to wow your clients and prospects.

Simple, yes? But I see so many business people wasting those golden opportunities. Just think how many opportunities you have to do something different, something that will make your client or prospect say 'wow'.

- The envelope in the post
- Your stationery
- The way you answer the telephone
- Your email footer (or lack of)

- Your website
- Your business card

Every contact point is an opportunity that cries out for you to say something about your business, your values, your style, your ethos and how much you care about your clients or your prospects.

Go on. Have a closer look at your own stuff. My guess is you'll be underwhelmed.

A WARM WELCOME - OR NOT?

Picture this. You have a precious new prospect coming to see you at your business premises. The meeting is in your diary, you've confirmed the time, now you're sitting patiently, waiting for them to arrive, ready to explode your sales pitch and convert your unsuspecting victim. You intend to make an impact.

What if there was another way to make an impact on your prospective client, one that starts even before you shake hands? It's simply a system. A system that you could easily put in place to ensure that your prospect is wooed from the moment the meeting is set up to the moment you finish your opening proposal to them. The system costs nothing, is easy to implement and will knock their socks off. It looks like this.

One of your team takes responsibility for every prospect meeting. When a meeting is arranged, and as soon as it's in the diary, a *'You've got a date'* postcard is sent out to confirm the time and location.

A confirmation of the meeting is emailed to the

We've got a date...

...a sincere commitment to growing your business!

RussellPayne&Co
ask for more, get more.

a sincere commitment to growing your business

RUSSELL PAYNE & Co.
CHARTERED ACCOUNTANTS

a sincere commitment to growing your business
step out of the ordinary...

Dear

We look forward to seeing you

at _____

on _____

with _____

If you need to rearrange this appointment, please call
us on 01522 533588 or email info@russellpayne.co.uk

A sincere commitment to growing your business.

prospect simultaneously, with a Google map of the location and directions attached. This means there can be no misunderstanding around the date or time and your prospect knows exactly how to find you.

On the day of the meeting, the potential client drives into your car park and sees a prominently placed A-board welcoming them by name and offering them exactly what they need: *This car parking space is reserved for...* That's it. The attention to detail speaks volumes.

I can't count the number of times that a potential client has been blown away by this simple process. In fact, I know that one prospect was so bowled over by this personal touch that they telephoned their partner to tell them all about their unexpected welcome.

Small gesture: huge impact. Your prospective client now knows that you've prepared for them, thought about their needs and taken some action to make their day easier. All before they've even crossed your threshold.

By the way, our long-term clients also look out for their personalised A-board when they pop in for a meeting. In fact, they've been known to complain if there isn't one waiting for them, even when the visit was spontaneous and we didn't know they were coming!

So, if you have a car park, it will cost you very little

time, effort or money to put a similar process in place. If you want to wow your clients and prospects, it's a no-brainer.

Choose 'Wow', not 'Ow'!

PLEASE WIPE YOUR FEET

Branding, including little corporate gifts and giveaways, can be overdone and, in my mind, many freebies are tacky and only serve to demonstrate the lack of thought and imagination about how to woo a prospect. Our office kitchen cupboard is full of thick ungainly mugs from various banks, image consultants and, particularly for some reason, recruitment agencies. It's only the hoarder in me that stopped me throwing them into the bin immediately.

Cheap branded, giveaway pens find no place on my desk and I feel vaguely insulted that anyone would think that a free pen will be the clincher for me to do business with them over the years to come. It is pathetic to believe that a little pen will make any difference at all and if it does, you're targeting the wrong clients.

Think about it. Mugs, umbrellas, pens, notepads, pencil sharpeners, little furry things that stick to computers, the list is endless and pointless. Blah, blah, blah...

There are better ways to use your precious logo which, let's not forget, represents the values and quality of your business. For example, instead of a traditional 'Welcome' doormat, why not go for one with your logo on it? Branding ideas should be unusual, clever or fun and certainly our 'own-brand' doormat has been a source of amusement over the years. For one thing, it keeps getting pinched but, eventually, the thieves realise it's daft to use a doormat with somebody else's name on it and, believe it or not, each time it disappears it mysteriously reappears several days later.

Think outside the box. We found a fantastic company in Holland that uses recycled metal to produce very fancy paperclips. Now, that is different. The quality is great and the fact that they are made from recycled materials fits well with our business ethics. They are used time and time again and, although not cheap at the outset, they say something about our business and they'll be around forever.

Thinking up new ideas is not as easy as picking out something from a catalogue and slapping your logo on it, but originality will make you more memorable, which is exactly what you want. Creative ideas might not be your thing but you could ask members of your team to take on the challenge. You might find that they relish the idea of thinking up original, alternative ideas and will see the task as an opportunity to contribute something more to the business.

It's very challenging, but fun.

WORLD CLASS DREAMING

About 10 years ago I went to a workshop in a hotel near Heathrow airport and the speaker for the three-day event was the wonderful Michael E. Gerber, author of the invaluable The E-Myth Revisited: Why Most Small Businesses Don't Work and What to Do About It.

I had no idea why the workshop was called The Dreaming Room but it was intriguing, so I took the train to London, anticipating a great event and hoping for the transfer of some astonishing business wisdom from Mr Gerber.

On the first morning, Michael Gerber walked in and said: 'Ok fellas, what's your dream? I am going to leave the room for 20 minutes and let you think about it and, when I come back, you can share your dreams with everybody in the room.'

Twenty minutes later Michael returned. I am not particularly slow in coming forward and, of course, I immediately volunteered to vomit my dream onto everybody else.

'Go on Russell, let's have it,' said our guru. Grinning widely, I proudly stood up and said I wanted to run a world-class accountancy practice.

'Wow,' he retorted. 'Is that it?'

It was. Then, in a very straightforward and measured manner, over the next couple of days Michael explained exactly how everyone present could build a world-class business. It turned out that it was just a step-by-step process. He took us through the steps that would lead us to a world-class business. Although, at the time, I wasn't totally chuffed with the process, I did see his point.

The steps will be slightly different according to business type. I'm not going to take you through each one right now – read Michael's book – but, in essence, he spoke about the following key business areas that it's essential to get right if you want your business to grow and develop into your world-class dream.

- Pricing
- Customer service
- Getting paid
- Motivating the team
- Mapping your results
- Goal setting
- Corporate identity

I mean, let's face it, what else is there? Michael gave

us a valuable lesson when he reminded us that becoming world class is about the effort, innovation and processes you put into your business. It means working on your business instead of in your business. No matter who you are or what type of business you have, to be able to call your business world class is a dream that is very much achievable. It's something that you could be proud of when you are tucked away in that brown box and the congregation is singing hymns, followed by your eulogy! We're going to look at some of these processes a little further in.

So come on! The decision to be world class is yours to make.

GIVE 'EM SOMETHING TO WORK WITH

Do you feel sorry for the editor of your local newspaper? You should. Local businesses give them such rubbish to talk about.

Picture the scene. It's Monday morning. Our reporter fires up her email and a dozen press releases immediately appear onscreen. The seasoned reporter instantly recognises the names of businesses that she has previously received so-called 'news releases' from. If they were useful to her in the past – that is, they offered her an interesting story and were appropriate to the newspaper's readership – she will open the email and scan the first couple of sentences. Ten seconds – that's all the time you have to make an impact.

If, on the other hand, our reporter sees the names of businesses that have sent her poorly written, inappropriate, uninteresting news releases in the past, she will probably just delete them and move on to something more promising.

The news desk is inundated with naff, pointless, uninteresting stories of happenings in the local community that, thankfully, we never read about.

You know how it goes... the local firm of accountants has a NIB (news in brief) about Gerald Tweedbottom's elevation to the status of partner having spent 45 years with the firm as a senior manager. Well done, Gerald. Really interesting read. The only reason why this fascinating item appeared is probably because the firm in question spends a small fortune advertising in the newspaper.

Meanwhile, the story about how the same firm has raised thousands of pounds for charity is untold. Because no one in the company thinks it's newsworthy. Which story is most interesting to the reader and most valuable to the business? It's the one that shows prospective clients that you're ethical, caring and human. And this story wouldn't cost you a penny in advertising. Get writing.

Trust me, there are plenty of things happening in your lives and businesses that are newsworthy.

Think outside the box. If you can't think of anything, ask your staff. If you still can't see the wood for the trees, speak to a professional.

I promise you, the editor of your local newspaper would be delighted if you could use your loaf, just a little bit, and make it easy for them to say yes to your story.

So, think or stink!

TGI FRIDAY OR TGI MONDAY?

If you are in business and all you're looking forward to is 5pm on Friday evening, you've made a big mistake somewhere along the line.

Steve Jobs used to say: "If I wake up five days in a row and I can't say to myself, 'I love what I am doing', I know something has to change." He was right. If you set up a business and what you do doesn't turn you on Monday to Friday, you need to take a look at yourself and your business.

If your service or product doesn't light the blue touchpaper for you then, it's unlikely to do it for your customer either. So ask yourself honestly, do you dread Mondays or are you so eager to get to work that you bounce out of bed whistling?

I have helped a huge number of business owners over the past 25 years and in many cases what's taken the fun out of being in business is not the product, trade or service, it's simply the way that the business has been set up or the way it has evolved over the years. At some point in the journey, the fire has gone out, the early excitement and enthusiasm has drained away and you've let your business become predictable. And it's hard to get fired up over the same old, same old.

TGI Monday?

If underneath it all, you really do love and believe in what you do, then the rest can be fixed.

Although it may feel like it at times, there probably aren't 679 things wrong with your business, it's usually just a case that a few basic principles around how you run your business have gone astray.

Namely:

- Your customer service (or lack of it)
- Your pricing policy (or lack of it)
- Your ability to get paid in good time (or lack of it)
- Your overall business strategy (or lack of it)

It doesn't get much simpler than that.

A positive attitude may not solve all of your problems, but it will annoy enough people to make it worthwhile!

TIN OR BIN?

I can't remember exactly where I heard this idea and, of course, there are several different versions. It's all about grading your clients or customers. The best categorisation I have come across is Platinum, Gold, Silver, Bronze, Tin... and Bin!

We're all familiar with the 80/20 rule and its derivatives. And we all know, don't we, that putting lipstick on a pig doesn't fool anyone and that it's impossible to polish a turd – although I know you can roll it in glitter...

The key to true categorisation of your clients is to let them know in which category they sit.

It isn't surprising that platinum clients are going to be the ones you like the most. You really enjoy working with them and they are probably some of your most profitable clients. There is no harm in that. It makes sense for you to encourage your Bronze clients to aspire to Silver, your Silver to Gold and the Gold to join the ranks of the Platinum. Inevitably the Tin and bin clients are going to find their way out of your life one way or another - either you do it or they do it.

My experience is that clients love to know what category they are in and I've had many a joke with clients about them being 'only Bronze'.

But here's a word of warning. When the Platinum client says jump, you jump! They are your all singing, all dancing clients, so you have to be their all singing, all dancing provider. Make sure they have your mobile phone number and offer them 24/7 support. Nobody rings at 3am on a Sunday, but just letting them know they could, if need be, is value indeed.

Most business owners have Tin clients, even though they sometimes find it hard to admit. Tin clients are slow payers (sometimes never paying), they will take every opportunity to moan about something and they never, ever, blame themselves for the poor performance of their own business. It is always someone else's fault - and often they'll say it's yours! Get rid of them as soon as you can.

Which brings me to something that I picked up at a marketing workshop run by my friend, Peter Thomson (www.peter.thomson.com) It's called DDWT.

I had never heard it before but I have used it hundreds of times since and it always gets lots of laughs at my Bootcamps - because DDWT means Don't Deal With Tossers. Cheeky, but entirely appropriate. There are some people and businesses that you really don't want to be involved with.

DDWT is a mantra that every business owner seeking success should live by. If every morning when you get out of bed, you tell yourself today will be another day when I DDWT I promise you that slowly but surely your business will become easier and more fun to run.

Guaranteed.

USE IT OR LOSE IT

Did you ever receive an email from someone and, as a result, wanted to telephone them rather than email them by return?

Yes? I find it happens a lot. It's mind numbing. Of course, if you want to send an email back you just hit 'reply' and, if you want to pick up the phone, all you have to do is scroll to the bottom of the email to find their contact telephone number. Yes? Well, all too frequently that's a 'no'.

Yep, sometimes there are no contact details at all and the email simply finishes with a cheerful 'best regards, Geoff'.

Even worse, and something that I think is particularly insulting, is the abbreviated sign off - a strangulated 'Bst Rgds, Geoff'. Now, does 'Geoff' have such a busy life that he can't even be arsed to use vowels? Does 'Geoff' think I'm not worth the time it takes to include three vowels in his email sign off? Hmm. It begs the question – does 'Geoff' really want my business?

Your email footer is a fantastic opportunity to showcase yourself, your business, your product and

Never wrestle with a pig, you get dirty and besides, the pig loves it!

your news without the customer or prospect having to go to your website to learn more. Anyone who isn't adding value to their emails by using a well-crafted, informative footer is throwing away numerous opportunities to engage, interest and attract clients or customers.

In the vast majority of businesses, people buy people and, behind that, they buy the product. I really believe that is the order. You only get out what you put in and when you do the little things well, you will win and retain the loyalty of your customer. Your email signature and footer is a discrete and effective opportunity to show your personality, your values and your business ethos – repeatedly.

Why not add a colour photograph of yourself in the footer? If you are selling a personal service, it could build rapport and add a sense of intimacy. And if you happen to be at the same networking event one day you'll immediately be able to match the face to the name. Or take the opportunity to include some of your corporate branding and your strapline if you have one - and if you haven't, work on it and get one. Again, I'll come on to branding and straplines.

Make sure all the information in your email footer is relevant. Run the content by a friend or someone in your team to check that it's accurate, spelt correctly and looks professional.

Here's one more thing about email. If your email address looks like this -
katiessmith1994@completebusinesssolutions.co.uk
it's time you looked for an alternative format. It's

too long, it's too hard to remember, and it's wide open to mis-spelling. Most domains will offer variations of your email address, for example, the above email could easily be shortened to katiesmith@cbs.co.uk

Think about all the ways that you can make it easier to help your customers do business with you – then make them happen.

Use all your chances or lose them.

Expert Insert

GET IT 'WRITE' FIRST TIME

We've all seen shockingly amateur advertisements in the local press or flyers that look like a dog's breakfast. Mis-spelt, badly worded, featuring a heavy use of unprofessional fonts, dull photography or unfunny cartoon images - they all shout out the same thing - 'I did it myself to save a bit of money'!

Unless you're a skilled writer as well as an entrepreneur, you're unlikely to be able to dash off some sparkling copy for a press release at the drop of a hat, or be able to pull together a punchy and inviting marketing or advertising campaign over a quick coffee. So why waste your time?

Freelance writer Janet Marshall has decades of experience of writing for businesses and knows what a difference clear, articulate and easy to read text can make to a website, marketing email or brochure.

One of the talents of a good business owner is the ability to know when to call in the professionals. Few things are more important than promoting your business through the wide range of digital, print and media channels. The way you present your business goes before you, even before you shake the hand of a prospective client or customer, through your publicity and advertising.

So use the professionals to write, edit and produce creative images and ideas for your business. Compared to the boost to your income that a well thought out and successful marketing campaign will net, the costs of using a freelance will be minimal. And at the same time, working with a professional will be a great learning opportunity and will increase your knowledge of what makes a marketing campaign great.

Find Janet at Writing Life
Janetmarshall.wordpress.com

THE THREE BIG LIES

Can I remember? Oh yes. 'I love you', 'the cheque is in the post', and... damn it, I can't remember the third one. Never mind, let's put the wonderful world of romance to one side for now and have a closer look at 'the cheque is in the post'.

In business we have to make a profit. If not, ultimately, it will all be over. And many a business has gone into liquidation through lack of cash rather than lack of profit.

When I set up in business in 1991 you needed only two things to be a client of mine - a pulse and a chequebook. At that time, when a new client came along my only thought was 'yippee!' It was a new client and it didn't matter that they might be slow to play or, indeed, might never pay. I didn't care. It was another client and that was good enough for me at the time.

I then spent the next 15 years of my business running around like a headless chicken, chasing cash or cheque payments from my clients. It was so long ago I can't even remember what terms of payment were on the invoices I sent out, but nobody took any notice of them anyway so what was the point?

Then, in about 2005, I had a brainwave. Another light bulb moment. I realised that if I could persuade all my clients to pay by monthly standing order, they would be able to spread their payments - which makes it easier for them - and my cash would also come in monthly, giving me a steady cash flow. We could all benefit. Bingo!

It seemed like a great idea at the time, but as more and more clients changed to a monthly standing order, my bank statements started to grow and I ended up with a seven-page monthly statement showing every single payment from each individual client. It was rapidly becoming an administrative and internal bookkeeping nightmare.

Then, in a defining moment in 2008, somebody introduced me to the Direct Debit scheme. Yes, that obvious form of receiving payment which had been used for years by all the financial institutions and utility companies to collect your money each month, on the due date – and my admin nightmare ended.

Direct Debits transformed the way we managed our cash flow. From that point onwards, our existing or new client signed an authority to enable us to collect by Direct Debit and away we went. It couldn't have been easier.

The only report I receive highlights defaults – if any clients happen not to pay. Meanwhile, the facilitating DD company collects all the monthly instalments on my behalf and the cash comes into my business account twice monthly, levelling out the cash flow throughout the year.

I repeat, this is probably one of the most important

things I have ever implemented in my own business. Since then, I've also helped dozens of my clients to implement the DD scheme in their businesses with great success – and it's revolutionised their cash flow too.

It can for you, too.

HERE! HERE!

It's true. You don't know what you don't know.

A while back, I was in an email dialogue with a golfing pal of mine, Ken Tunstall. I can't remember what the subject matter was but Ken had emailed me concerning his views on the matter at hand and I'd responded with a supportive 'Here, Here!'

Back came the comment...

'I think you'll find it's 'Hear! Hear!' old chap!'

What? I prepared a witty riposte that began:

'Ken, for a start, I am not old - you are! And you are a crap golfer!' Then I paused, opened up Google and typed 'here, here'. Yes, there it was. Ken was absolutely right and I once again had to eat humble pie and stand corrected. However, he is still a crap golfer.

Where am I going with this sorry tale? It's this. Sometimes you have to admit that you don't know everything. I'm always amazed that perfectly sensible business owners who are great at what they do try to cut corners within their business, such as by creating their own websites.

Your website is probably the first place that your customers and prospects go to once you've managed to connect with them face-to-face, via an email marketing campaign or, preferably, through the direct recommendation of a satisfied customer.

Naturally, they want to see what you're offering them. And you want them to be impressed.

Now, in my experience, most small business websites are, at best, average. Why? Because too few business owners use professionals to design and write their websites. As a result, websites are either deadly dull or crammed with every gimmick possible. Images – if there are any - are often no better than snapshots and, content-wise, they may be poorly written with copy that is not optimised for the web and obviously hasn't been proofread or sense checked.

I have been working for several years with two superb proof reading and copy specialists. Freelance writer Janet Marshall (janetmarshall.wordpress.com) and Elena Munns (bespokepa.co.uk) have helped me by proof reading and creating copy for marketing material and, beyond that, by going through client and prospect websites with a fine toothcomb to eliminate errors and sense check them.

Creating a readable, attractive business website is a 'critical non-essential' that few business owners take enough time to think through. However, it's your virtual shop front and may be the deciding factor for potential clients or customers thinking of doing business with you. If you don't get your own stuff right, they won't trust you with theirs.

You don't know what you don't know - but you can find a professional to advise you.

AH! THAT'S INTERESTING...

The idea of going to a networking event is to pick up business. That's why they call it networking - not netplaying. You should move around the room as effectively and as quickly as possible and pick up as many business cards as you possibly can in the time allowed, then work out who you are serious about doing business with.

Do you then go back to your desk and go through the stack of business cards you've acquired and then, one by one, chuck them in the bin? Or do you dutifully file them away? In fact, get your business card file out now and - never mind the quantity - look at the quality. How interesting are they?

Yes, there's a business name, address, company name, phone number, email address, website address blah, blah. All the contact details you could possibly want are there. But there's something missing...

Ask yourself, how many cards have personality? What makes a business card - and the person who gave it to you - stand out? Maybe it's a different size or shape? It could show an image of the person who gave it to you. Did it feel thicker or more textured than others? Did it have a great logo or interesti

Those of you hoping to attend our Managing Disappointment seminar, we are sorry to say it has been cancelled... again.

strapline that told you something more about their business? Maybe it used an intriguing 'call to action'?

If you print your business cards in the thousands think again. Just take a little time out to be different. Ask a graphic designer to play around with some ideas - there's nothing they love more than the challenge of producing something original and interesting - and don't settle for a logo that looks like a cheap tattoo, especially if it's the one you've had for years. That logo represents your business and it probably makes more of an impact than your name or your sparkling business chat up line.

How about a strapline? That's a tough call. In my experience, although you may have landed on a catchy strapline that perfectly reflects your ethos and your product offering, you'll be bored with it after a few years. Find another way to give your ethos a fresh expression. It's time to sit down and brainstorm.

I think it was Winston Churchill who said 'To improve is to change: to be perfect is to change often'. It's the same with your corporate identity and branding: keep it fluid, keep it fresh, keep it moving.

Take a notepad now and scribble out a few ideas for your next fabulous strapline.

ARE YOU RESPONSIVE?

Of course, you all know that Google has started to penalise those websites that aren't responsive by lowering the site's SEO ranking? That's right. If your website isn't mobile-friendly, or isn't properly configured for smartphones, your rankings on Google search will have dropped.

Responsive in this sense means that your website is designed to automatically give consumers an optimised view of your website on smartphones and tablets. Do you know that 74% of consumers will only wait five seconds for a web page to load on their mobile device before abandoning the site? Or that 71% of mobile browsers expect web pages to load almost as quickly or faster than web pages on their desktop computers?

It doesn't have to cost thousands and most web developers would recommend that you optimise your website, particularly if you are selling online. Affordable, necessary and advisable.

Maybe the bigger question is whether your website is working hard enough for you? When was the last time you checked out competitor sites? And you are measuring your website's analytics, aren't you?

Depending on the type of business you have, here are some things you should consider having on your website:

- Video – consumers love it
- 360 degree photography – shows off your products from every angle
- A blog – regular, unique, quality content will help you rise up the SEO ranks as well as raise your business profile with customers
- Testimonials from happy customers or clients – third party recommendations help to build trust

A QR code can also help to bring more people to your website – ask your web developer. Use it in your marketing material or advertisements where it can be scanned by smartphones and take the user straight to the product they're interested in. Here's something else for you - it's called augmented reality and it's a 3D application based on a QR code. Go to Google or YouTube and search for 'augmented reality boot'. It's amazing, and although it may not be exactly what you need right now, it shows the endless possibilities of the web.

Don't be left behind. If you're not turned on by web stuff, find someone who is and ask them to keep you up to date with new developments.

Come on. Catch up!

CORPORATE VIDEO... YUK!

We've all had it drilled into us about how much Google likes video content. It's true, it does. But there's video and there's... well, let me explain further.

If you're feeling a bit low, I can recommend nothing better to cheer you up than to go to Google and type in, for example, accountants in Birmingham - although any random town will do.

Go through the sites and notice the differentiating, ground-breaking Unique Selling Points (USPs) that will make you salivate at the thought of what you'll find if you click through to their website to make contact.

You know the stuff:
'We take accountancy a step further'
'We also offer much more... tax, VAT, Will Planning'
'Our mission is to grow your business'

'For all your accounting needs'
'Need help with your accounts?'
'Expertise and specialisms in all tax and accounting'
You'll hardly be able to contain yourself.

A few of them - but only a few - will have video content. Click on the link and enjoy! Listen to a couple of minutes of drivel and then click on another. You can almost imagine that the same video production team made them.

But let's not blame the production team, usually it's the business owner that is scared - or unable - to think outside the box.

Usually, but not always.

Some firms, yes, even accountants, like to think outside the box. Take a look at the nutters at www.cassons.co.uk. I'm not being disrespectful here - one of the directors is a friend of mine and his name is actually Les Nutter.

Click on *Cassons, the movie* and enjoy. What fun they must have had putting it together. And does it set them apart? You're not kidding.

You can find another gem at www.rspartnership.co.uk.
They recruited a professional video company and their own team acted in the video - apart from the frustrated taxpayer who is looking for some help! Brilliant stuff. The only problem with such a fantastic offering is that they make it very difficult for the rest of us to follow, as the bar has been set so high.

Now there's a challenge.

I've recently done some great video work with a Lincoln firm called Wallbreaker – to see it, visit www.wallbreaker.co.uk and click on *Showreel*.   In particular, you'll find that their time-lapse video and corporate work is top notch.

Go on, do it! And, by the way, do it often because there's nothing worse than a website that plays the same old video time and time again, year after year.

Please, don't bore your customers.

Expert Insert

Say 'no' to corporate monotony

The trouble with most corporate videos is that they can be formal to the point of dull. But, if you're a small business trying to make a name for yourself in a highly competitive market you need something fresh and original that will make an impact on sophisticated internet consumers.

Wallbreaker Productions is a Lincoln-based company that specialises in creating imaginative digital videos that capture the personality, flair and style of a business.

Luke Winter, Ashley Wilks and Thomas McKie set up Wallbreaker with the aim of breaking the walls of corporate video monotony. Their technical and creative know-how takes seemingly dull business concepts and turns them into stunning, original videos that communicate their clients' products, services and ethos.

'It's easy for businesses to stick to tried and tested visual concepts,' says Wallbreaker Producer Ashley Wilks. 'Videos can be expensive and we understand that it can be a significant cost for a small business, so they will naturally be cautious.

'We recommend that any business considering using video in their digital marketing mix should shop around to find a professional production company with a wide portfolio of work. The company you choose should demonstrate that it can produce work that is fresh and original and you should feel confident that they understand your market and needs.

'At Wallbreaker, we work closely with our clients to develop creative, eye-catching videos that grab the attention. We deliver videos with high quality production values that will really work hard for them on their websites and on channels such as YouTube and Facebook, ensuring that our clients receive a good return on their investment, both in terms of generating sales as well as promoting awareness of their company within their market.'

Check them out at www.wallbreaker.co.uk.

GET READY FOR THE OLYMPICS!

The business development books that you buy at the airport before jetting off on holiday would almost certainly have a section on goal setting. Why? That's simple. It's because goal setting is proven time and time again to be the most effective way of achieving targets.

If you ask most business owners what their goals are their answers will probably be along the lines of:

- To make enough money to pay the bills at the end of the month
- I suppose it would be nice to grow the business
- We are going to try and make more money so we can move up the property chain
- Well, the goal is to make more money this year because the kids are off to university shortly
- If I can make enough money to have a new car every three years, that would be great
- I would like to be busier but the market is so competitive
- We're trying to work out a way to be cheaper than the competition

How can I put this politely? These are not goals, they're half-hearted wishes and dreams.

When you set real goals, you put some real plans behind them. Most of us have heard of SMART goals, but few adopt them and make them work for their business. What does a SMART goal look like? Like this:

Specific – it's a clearly expressed and focused goal
Measurable – you can quantify what success means
Achievable – but it will probably challenge you, in a good way
Realistic – it's not just a daydream
Time bound – you have to work to a deadline

Let's look at SMART goals in more detail. First, what use is a goal that's easy to achieve? It won't motivate you, it won't challenge you, and it won't force you to innovate. In fact, you won't have to do anything over and above what you're already doing. How rewarding will that be?

If you truly want to be SMART you need to set yourself a target. It could be anything that will move your business forward, for example, greater turnover, higher profit, more employees, or a greater number of new products. No matter what, find a goal that is challenging and will really motivate you, so that, when you achieve your goal in the timeframe you set out, it will give you massive personal satisfaction. In achieving that goal, you will also know that you've improved the value and performance of your business, and that has to be good all round, especially for anyone who's considering an exit strategy.

Now, to the Olympics.

I promise you that, whenever you are reading this book, it will be a maximum of four years until the next Olympics. So, maybe now is a good time to set an 'Olympic Goal' for your business. Work out what the goal is, brand it as your Olympic Goal, and share it with everyone in your team and your customers and prospects. Be proud of it, live it, breathe it - do it. And endeavour to achieve it by the next Olympics!

Let me tell you, goal-setting works. I moved into some superb new offices in 2008, in the teeth of the recession, taking on significantly larger office overheads at a time when my market for clients and prospects was shrinking, especially in the construction industry. We set an Olympic Goal to double the company turnover by the time of the London Olympics, which at that time were 32 months away. I gathered everyone in the team around the table and I shared with them my aspirations to grow the business and to grow it significantly. Our Olympic Goal was born and everyone was keen to be a part of it.

The London Olympics took place in August 2012 and I have to report that we failed. By one month. We actually broke through our turnover target one month later than planned, in September 2012, by which time we'd doubled the size of the business in four years of deep recession.

I think we proved that, if the need is great enough, anything is possible. But you must gather the right strategic partners around you and apply common sense together with a clear strategy. You must be **SMART.**

Nobody has to do this stuff. If you don't want to grow your business, if you don't want it to be more valuable, if you don't want it to be more profitable, then, hey ho, just stay as you are.

It's your call.

Here's another good tip. Only floss the teeth you want to keep.

CHEAP AS CHIPS

At a Business Bootcamp I gave in Sheffield back in November 2013, I was slaughtered on the feedback form by two attendees who left after only 30 minutes of the scheduled four-hour event. Why? Because I recommended employing apprentices.

I had been talking about the inability of business owners to delegate day-to-day duties efficiently within their organisation. I was speaking from experience. I had been the major bottleneck in my own business and because of the stress and frustration that came as a result, I decided many years ago to delegate the responsibility of handling all of my clients to my senior team. It changed the way I ran my business.

Yes, I hear you say, 'that's all very well if you've got somebody to delegate to'. That was exactly the point I'd been making when my audience suddenly decreased by two.

The Government introduced the Apprenticeship Scheme with a view to taking young people out of college and into work. For most business owners who are trying to run a business and make some money, the minimum wage is a pretty hefty investment for a young student who comes green from college, maybe with some IT and Excel spreadsheet skills, but no real experience of work or

Apprentices:
cheap as chips.

knowledge of what it takes to run a business. At the minimum wage, taking on someone who needs to be trained, coached and developed, by you or one of your team, takes a good chunk out of £12,000 per annum plus management time, and if you are a small business of less than £200,000 turnover, it's a huge investment and one that's not without risk.

Taking on an apprentice is a lower investment and these youngsters need a chance to get on to the employment ladder. Yes, they earn a pittance for the first year of the apprenticeship - but they are like sponges when it comes to learning. Put some time aside and develop them. The more time you invest in your apprentices, the bigger the return on your investment. More importantly, at a very small cost, they give you the opportunity to delegate some of those tasks that you, the business owner, shouldn't be doing. Tasks such as answering the phone, preparing quotes, filing, creating spreadsheets and scanning or photocopying documents help apprentices understand how a business runs from the bottom up. It's a good grounding and will lead to greater things as they learn and develop with your help. But you, the business owner, should be focusing on other things, such as your business strategy, growing sales or improving your customer service.

I'm afraid the two ladies who exited the Bootcamp very early on just didn't get what I was trying to say. Business owners can massively increase the efficiency of their businesses by giving some youngsters a chance to get out into the business world.

Apprentices are a godsend.   Speak to your local college and find out more. You'll be welcomed with open arms and another young person could have a job and a step towards a good career.

They are worth their weight in gold.

SAME OLD, SAME OLD

Will somebody explain to me why it is so easy to see what is wrong with other businesses and yet the people running those businesses choose to do nothing about it?

Think about it. We all know what it feels like to enjoy brilliant customer service, in a restaurant, for example. You know it's a step-by-step, systemised process. It's how they answer the phone and whether they use the opportunity to take that 'extra step' at the first point of contact.

What would this extra step look like? It's all about thinking what your customer might need. So, when they ring to make a reservation, ask:

- Do you know how to find us?
- Have you been before?
- Can we send you directions by email?
- Are you celebrating anything? If so, would you like us to put some champagne on ice?

And so on and so on.

Some restaurants, but very few, do this brilliantly. If they have a system, it will work every time.

I've talked about customer service and how to take advantage of points of contact in other chapters, but although I refer to a restaurant here, the systems or processes that reflect the company's culture and values - 'the way we do things here' - apply to almost any type of business.

1%, 2%, 5% or 20% - IT COULD BE DISASTROUS NOT TO KNOW

My business development sessions with clients and prospects cover all aspects of business and our discussions are wide-ranging and frequently fascinating. But no session would ever be complete without spending time looking at the pricing levels within their business.

Our software, at www.pricesensitivity.co.uk, is an incredibly simple tool that I like to use to show the effects of product or service price increases on the profitability of a business, coupled with the potential loss of any customers who might choose to go elsewhere owing to a price increase. Altering the price upwards (never downwards) can show incredible improvement in results.

It comes back to the 'DDWT' advice that I mentioned earlier. If some people don't want to work with you at the right price for your product or service, then go out and find those who will. The right price is the level where you move further towards maximising the profitability of your business and your customer is still happy, perhaps even delighted, with the product or service you provide.

Nothing can ever be described as too expensive because, if it were truly too expensive, there would be no market for it.

Not many of us can afford a red Ferrari, but there is certainly a market for them, and a thriving one at that. What I am saying is, if you want to bring a premium product to the market, you should aim to obtain a premium price for it. It's a process of testing the market to establish that harmonious price point.

The great thing about pricing is, if you aim high, you can always come down to meet demand: you don't have to damage your market position indefinitely. By contrast, if you set your price too low and people are happy to buy, it is more difficult to increase your prices at a later date because you have already set expectations.

This is called top down selling, and it's a great habit to get into.

I have never met a business owner who didn't want to pay his team more, and the generation of profit within the business is the ultimate aim of most entrepreneurs and business owners. So don't leave money on the table by going in too low – unless, of course, it's a loss-leading project to acquire market share. That's a different argument altogether.

DON'T SHOOT THE MESSENGER

Today there's an overwhelming tendency to think that everything has to be digital and that's the only way to grow your business. Yes, digital platforms offer businesses amazing opportunities to interact with customers, but don't dismiss the traditional techniques out of hand.

The key is to test anything and everything.

I once had a terrible experience with a telemarketing company back in 2010. The company had come with a recommendation from a long-term friend but, unfortunately, turned out to be a real cowboy outfit. I think my friend's estimation of their performance had been too optimistic because what this company brought to my table was shambolic. In fact, it took me a few years to get over the experience and I swore never to use a telemarketing firm again.

However, we all know it's an aggressive market out there with everybody chasing each other's clients for business. So, in the spring of 2015, following the receipt of an email marketing campaign from another telemarketing firm, I put the bad memories behind me and gave it another go.

As it turned out, the new company did a superb job for me. If you are considering a telesales campaign

Don't shoot the
messenger.

carried out by a third party, I have some genuinely crucial advice, courtesy of Integrity Business Connections Ltd, which could help you to increase your level of success during your campaign.

The following rules proved to be incredibly valuable and significantly increased the results we achieved during and at the end of the telemarketing campaign they devised for us.

The rules are:

1. Only provide details for prospects you are serious about getting in front of. (Back to DDWT!).

2. If you end up in front of a 'tin or bin' prospect, don't blame the company doing the cold calling on your behalf.

3. Once a prospect meeting is arranged, follow up quickly and keep them warm.

4. Add them to your CRM database and keep them informed about what's happening in your business by whatever channels you normally rely on - email, newsletters, flyers or social media.

5. This helps to build your credibility before the eventual meeting, which may be weeks away, and in the meantime keeps your prospect warm and interested.

For some businesses, in some situations, this type of marketing still produces results. So consider including it in your marketing mix along with your digital channels, and give it a whirl.

Expert Insert

Enter the world of the 'mystery breaker'

If you've heard the term 'mystery breaker' before and wonder what it means, Austen Hempstead will tell you, because he is... a mystery breaker.

So what's the mystery? Well there's more than one according to Austen, but the typical mystery he breaks open often occurs when a company is under the illusion that their 'successful' sales people can sell. If your response is, 'hey, if they're making sales it proves they can sell', Austen offers a different interpretation of the facts.

'When a potential customer is in the market for a product or service, how many companies will the typical customer contact? Let's say three, including yours,' says Austen. 'Given that all three companies are selling a comparable product or service, the law of averages alone will enable your company to sell to one person in three. So, if your sales people sell to one in three, they're not 'selling', it's just the law of averages working for them.'

When sales are not happening at the expected level, many managing directors and sales directors think the solution is to tell their sales team to work harder. But selling is a skill, so if there's a problem with sales volumes it's usually a skill issue, not lack of effort.

Austen takes this issue right to the top. 'For a managing director or sales director to admit they don't know why sales are not on target isn't easy, but until they admit they don't have the answer, their company will struggle to develop and retain good sales people and the company won't reach its potential.

'I believe that we could increase GDP in this country exponentially if the majority of sales directors recognised that their role was akin to a manager of a sports team,' says Austen. 'A key part of their job is to help their people to become the best that they can be. And if that's not in their job description, it should be.'

Austen trains, develops and coaches sales people to become the best they can be and, in doing so, become a major asset to the company they work for.

Contact Austen at sellingisaskill.co.uk

PAPER CLICK MARKETING?

'Who is this dumb accountant who thinks pay per click marketing is 'paper click' marketing' I hear you say? Yes, I admit it - it's not that long since I first realised that pay per click had nothing to do with paper. In fact, when I wrote this chapter in July 2015, I didn't particularly care whether I was in the minority or majority of those who knew what it was.

What I did – and do - know for an absolute fact is that, if the majority know that PPC stands for Pay Per Click marketing, it is also true that only a minority of business owners are currently using it. But it's a form of marketing so effective, so cheap and so measurable, that most businesses should explore it to see whether it can indeed work for them.

Certainly, most business owners know that SEO stands Search Engine Optimisation and that it's about optimising your website and its contents to ensure that you have a good chance of appearing on page one or the early results pages for the most popular search engines, including Google, Yahoo and Bing. SEM, on the other hand, stands for Search Engine Marketing, which entails paying for your site to rank at the top of search engine pages – an internet advertisement in other words.

Each time someone clicks on your advertisement,

Even your paper clips send out a message...

russellpayne.co.uk

you will be charged - the Cost Per Click (CPC). The CPC of your ad depends on how narrow and specific your keywords are when trying to drive people to your website. For example, 'Accountants in England' would cost you an absolute fortune because it is such a wide search term, whereas 'Accountants in John O'Groats' - a phrase less often searched - would be less expensive and more cost effective.

There are three particularly fantastic aspects to PPC and these are as follows:

1. You can set a daily budget as low or as high as you like, and once that budget has been spent by people clicking on your advert, the ad is removed and you won't be charged further because people can no longer click through.

Unlike when you spend copious amounts of money advertising in newspapers, radio, or magazines, although you know the cost upfront, you have no idea how effective such adverts may turn out to be, so it's almost impossible to measure your return on investment.

2. Because you can monitor the click through rate, you can compare it to your daily budget to work out how much it is costing you for people to click through to your website. Then, of course, you can monitor the sales that accrue from a campaign and work out your exact Return On Investment.

3. You can turn your campaign on and off on a daily basis so there is no need to commit to a long-term contract or any of that nonsense. However, having said that, if you

prove that a PPC campaign is working, why would you switch it off if you can handle the demand?

It can be an absolutely brilliant tool, so it's worth exploring if it will work for you and your business. If it does, you've joined the minority of small business owners who dare to be different.

If you are looking for an expert, contact Alex Wright at knaptonwright.co.uk Alex had three years at Facebook and knows his stuff. Nice chap too!

This PPC marketing stuff works, it's an overwhelming minority who are using it. Have a play and see for yourself.

When you try
out new ideas,
accept that
you will make
misatkes.

GO ON, I DARE YOU!

Over the many years I've run my accountancy practice, I've seen thousands of businesses. I've seen a huge number of successful businesses that just do what they do very well, reliably and profitably in a well-oiled turnkey operation. I've also seen some amazing and innovative ideas that, unfortunately, never took off.

Of course, I've also seen some diabolical ideas in that time, but my overriding admiration is with those entrepreneurs who were brave enough to set out to be very different from the masses. To proudly raise your head above the parapet and claim to be different is a bold and profound statement. If, underneath all the paraphernalia, there truly is a different, innovative, idea, then a good accountant can help make their customers rich and profit nicely in the process.

Being innovative and thinking outside the box takes a lot of hard work - in fact, bloody hard work. I would go as far as to say that you need to have been in business for quite some time, and have felt the pain that comes from achieving only mundane results, mundane performance and customers who are at best merely satisfied, rather than delighted, to know how hard it can be.

The businesses that don't push the envelope tend to produce business results that look pretty much the same year after year - sometimes up, sometimes down, attracting a few new customers and losing a few. Not everyone is driven to push the boundaries through innovation, originality and customer service, and that's okay – for some.

For the rest, if your innovative idea doesn't excite or interest you, it certainly won't make an impact in the market place, where there is huge competition and variety of choice.

So, what are you going to do to make them choose you?

Well, before you even start thinking of making your processes more efficient so that you can clip a few pence off your cost of sales, stop! You're going nowhere fast. If your USP is that you are a bit cheaper than anybody else, then you will only have a business until somebody finds a way to do it cheaper than you - and trust me, somebody will. The investment of time and money that goes into driving down your costs is usually money unwisely spent compared to spending money on creating new ways to innovate and grab more market share.

Success is categorically not about the price of your product. I would much rather you raised your prices through upgrading your packaging to make it appear more desirable, or make more money by up-selling to those precious people who already buy your products and services.

If you truly believe that your product or service is the best, the most effective, or the highest quality, you need to direct your focus to making your product the must-have item or your company the go-to experts. You will need to do a lot more than redesign your logo and find a new strapline to achieve this - although that might be a good start.

Look at the great examples all around you - Apple and Virgin to name just two - and study how they use innovation and great marketing to achieve and sustain premium prices in crowded markets. They were once small businesses with big ideas. They had little money, but big imaginations. They had few employees, but big aspirations. If they did it, so can you.

Go on, I dare you.

CHEER UP, ONE DAY IT WILL ALL BE OVER!

The wonderful Michael E. Gerber, author of *The E-myth Revisited*, used to call it your 'clap out date'; that's when you pop your clogs and end up in that brown box.   At best, your COD is an estimate. Thankfully, not many of us know exactly how long we have left, so we may as well get on with it. But if you're in business on your own account, you at least have the opportunity to turn it into a business of real worth that you can leave to your family, sell to someone else or follow some other planned exit strategy.

So, the more you work on the systems within your business to ensure that, ultimately, it can run without you, the more you will increase its value. Whatever your exit strategy may be, that's smart thinking.

Too many people build a business to earn just enough money to pay the bills, pay off the mortgage and put some savings aside. They don't think about building a business – creating an asset – that, one day, they will be able to sell before retiring and living comfortably off the proceeds, or choose to simply live off the passive income that a successful business

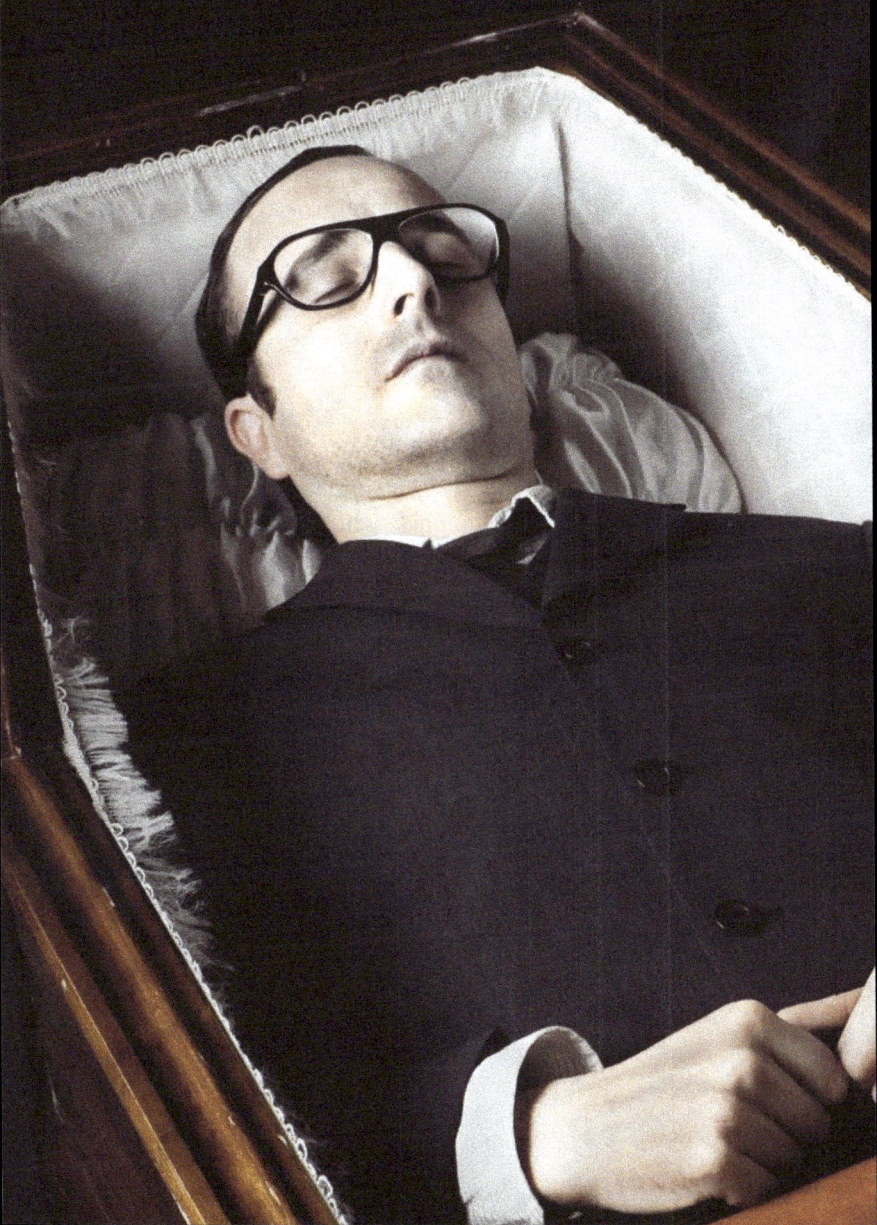

Cheer up, one day it will all be over.

can create for the rest of their lives.

Many people will say that they are in business, but when you look closely, it's just them - and only them - and when they are ill or on holiday, they stop earning. That's not a business, it's a job.

To build a business beyond your micro business you need to think about delegating, training and empowering. I think the key word there is delegation, but if you're on your own you have nobody to delegate to. And if you can't get rid of the mundane tasks within your business, you have no capacity to grow.

'Ah yes, but it's so risky taking on employees and trainees,' I hear you say. You are not wrong! But if you don't take the plunge you won't grow, you won't become more profitable and you certainly won't be able to build a business you can sell, so get over it and take the plunge. If you then find that the trainee, apprentice or school leaver is not developing as quickly as you hoped, before you let them go and go back to square one yourself, have a look at the training you've been giving them. Ask yourself whether you are giving them the best possible chance to develop - or is the problem that you've abdicated responsibility for that process?

Of course, you know how to run your micro business, but unless you show other people how to run it, your business will stay micro. There is nothing more satisfying than seeing people responding to investment, training and empowerment. Yes, you may make some mistakes when you employ people, but some will absolutely fly and bring new ideas, innovations and energy to your business. It is so uplifting to see how they can move your business forward – if you are open to change and challenge.

If they make mistakes, help them to learn from them. Remember that you once made mistakes. The more mistakes they make, the quicker they will learn. It will free you up to grow the business and build up your asset.

The Olympics are never more than four years away, so why don't you set an Olympic Goal and commit yourself to take on some new people to train and empower by the next Olympics?

If you don't, when your 'clap out date' arrives both you and your business will be history.

ABOUT US

I know this chapter will sound like a mind-numbing rant; if it does, I've got my message across. It's meant to be.

In fact, test this out for yourself. Go to a search engine, pick out 10 random websites and then click on the 'about us' tab that will inevitably be at the top of the homepage somewhere.

The vast majority of the time the 'about us' section will have absolutely nothing, or at best very little, of interest to read about the people who founded and work within the business. Unless the business is employing robots, this couldn't be further from the truth, so why not have a bit of fun and show that your business has a personality.

People do business with people. Why not ask all your team members (and if you haven't got any team members, get some) to provide a short summary about themselves - who they are, what they do, what they like and maybe something about them that nobody else knows. Ask them to provide a photograph of themselves as a child or a baby and have your website designer set up the 'about us' page so your customers can hover over the photograph and see the adult appear. It is so easy to implement and I think you will find that you will receive compliments about it when your clients and

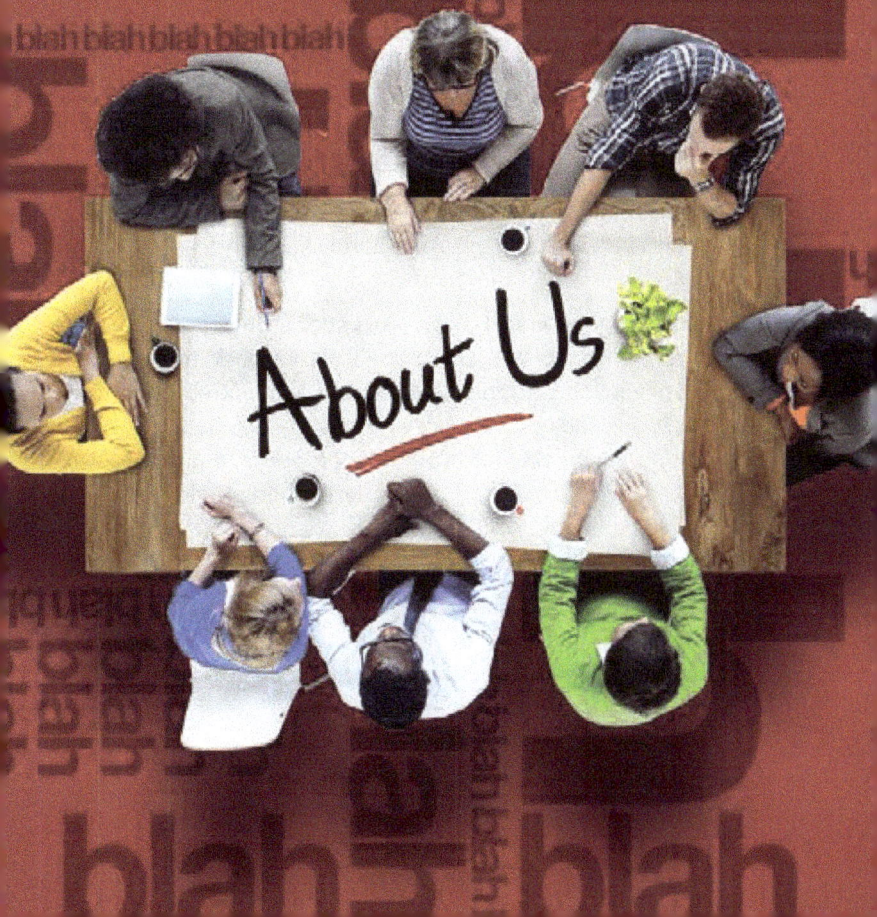

prospects engage with you.

There are plenty of alternative versions of the same idea out there. Be creative with artist's impressions, show you have a sense of fun and choose cartoon images of team members or display photos of the animal they'd most like to be.

Your business will stand out from those who stick to the bland 'contact us at' followed by an email address or phone number. And it will reveal more to your customers about your attitude, energy and values than reading about Joe Bloggs who's been in charge of credit control and order processing for 40 years. Boring, boring, boring!

It's so easy to bring life, colour and character to your business and make a big impact on your clients, and it takes very little expense and hardly any effort.

Yes, it's a good idea. So don't just stick it on your list of things to do and think you'll come back to it whenever you get time. It will never happen. Get the ball rolling today. And while you're at it, inject some life and personality into your email footer and put a flattering (but realistic) up to date photograph of yourself on there too.

Word of advice: don't use the best photograph you've ever had taken of yourself. You'll have to face insulting questions such as *'how long ago was that taken?'* forever after. I know.

Expert Insert

Social media – the clue's in the title

Running a social media marketing agency wasn't on my school careers officer's list: lawyer, doctor, accountant, commissions in the armed forces, yes, but working in more creative industries? No. That was largely because social media marketing hadn't been invented in 1997, but once it had arrived I grabbed it by the horns and made a living from it by helping other businesses do it well.

I have a great, sometimes unmanageable, interest in learning 'stuff'. I'm a voracious consumer – but, frustratingly, not always a retainer – of information: sports news, tech news, history, biographies and much more. I think this interest in the world we live in and what makes it tick plays an enormous role in my success in social media marketing. To understand how businesses can use online social networks as an effective marketing channel, a key part of their marketing mix, requires an appreciation of one crucial fact: everyone is different. This is nothing new in marketing, but transferring that across to social media seems to escape many marketers, business owners and business commentators.

Social media is an almost indefinable term, in reality. The OED has it as: "Websites and applications that enable users to create and share content or to participate in social networking." In my world, it covers the online representation of what humans, and animals, have been doing since time began: word of mouth messaging, sharing and interacting with each other. If you think of social media as purely an online phenomenon, you're missing its most important facet: content is predominantly created by people and people don't live in computers, much as it might appear they do.

People drive social media, and people drive me forward. A social media marketing agency must be based on two things: solid business foundations and fun. My business is run in partnership with my wife, much like my life as a whole! It is our goal to create a Silicon Valley style business that sits in the heart of Lincolnshire, providing talented people with a place they can do great work, have great fun and will recommend to their friends and connections.

Contact Alex at knaptonwright.co.uk

CAN YOU BE BOTHERED?

Over the past few years, I reckon I must have delivered around 30 Business Bootcamps at various locations throughout the UK.

The attendees listen with great enthusiasm as we go over ideas for business growth. Some of the ideas are relatively new, such as the growth in Pay Per Click marketing, but most of the ideas have been around for years and years, and yet business owners still fail to implement them.

One of the handouts we give at Business Bootcamp is entitled *My Bootcamp Top 10*, and this is an attempt to get the attendees to leave with at least 10 important actions that they will implement when they get back to their office, factories, home office or garden shed.

I suppose it's a compliment that often attendees come back to several Bootcamps, explaining that they always get something new from each one, but I'm afraid the harsh reality is that often their Bootcamp Top 10 is the same year on year. What I mean is, they make the same mistakes and take away the same ideas for action but fail to implement them effectively, if at all. It's the same old story.

Sometimes
those who need
it the most are
inclined the least.

People may be good at putting aside strategic time to work on their businesses and how they might thrust it forward with growth and increased profitability, and attending my Business Bootcamp is a perfect example. But as soon as they get back to the coalface and are dealing with the day-to-day issues and problems, innovation and strategy is pushed to the bottom of the pile. The longer it takes to implement, the less likely it is that the intended action will ever find its way into the business.

'Another day older is another day colder.'

How many times do we hear ourselves say 'now, that's a good idea' but, time and time again, we never get around to actually doing anything about it. Worse, the idea is only implemented on a short-term basis.

A few years ago I worked with a restaurant owner who loved my idea (or should I say somebody else's idea) of putting a little raffia ticket saying 'recommended wine of the week' around a particular bottle of wine in his restaurant. Of course, it was never a bottle of house wine but one of the more expensive choices on the wine menu - and it dramatically increased sales in the short term. That is to say, as long as the promotional tickets were used.

After having achieved really great results, there was a failure to systemise the idea, which meant the process of adding tickets to the wine bottles lasted for a month or two and then it quietly slipped out of the business without anybody noticing.

So FTS - failure to systemise - is just as useless as FTI - failing to implement.

Unless you develop a system within your business, it will happen randomly and only when you are driving it personally. In fact, try it. Implement a system that you are personally responsible for without explaining and clarifying to the whole team that this is a system to be implemented on a daily basis. Not randomly, but every day of the working week. Then try going on holiday for a couple of weeks and ask somebody to mystery shop your business and see whether the system operates while you are away. I think you'll find it will be a case of 'while the cat's away...'

Your idea is systemised and embedded in your business or it isn't. And if it isn't, it's only a short-term measure. And an opportunity lost.

THE CLOCK'S TICKING...

If you are going to wow your customers you need to find out what really irritates them.

If you dare to ask your customers and prospects the question, then, armed with that valuable information, you can do something about it.

Let's be honest, the accountant's annual fee is something of a grudge purchase. If people thought they could get by without an accountant I am sure they would so, to a certain extent, they are shoehorned into a position where they have to buy.

I would be the last person to say that an accountant cannot bring huge value in proactivity, but my gut feel is that, in the main, the vast majority of accountants are merely compliance accountants, counting the beans, working out the tax and issuing an annual bill that generally rises year on year.

Like most people, I have need of a solicitor's help from time to time because we can get into a lot of trouble without the proper guidance. But that too is still something of a grudge purchase and, for me, my rant is that I never know what it is going to cost me because solicitors won't generally work on a fixed fee. This means I experience that horrible feeling of

The clock's ticking...

the clock ticking at considerable hourly rates. It's one of those scenarios where we have to buy, without knowing what it will ultimately cost us.

This lack of certainty is always going to be a barrier to entry and any business owner who can clearly show what a product or service is going to cost, no strings attached and fully guaranteed, have an advantage in the market and a much stronger USP.

I suppose my gripe here is about the billing per hour that is used in most professional practices. Another mind-numbing rant, I guess, but the need to fill out timesheets in six-minute chunks is something that I find hugely irritating and I am sure that the vast majority of people out there buying into professional services would agree with me.

I have recently noticed that many legal firms are now offering fixed-fee divorces as a package, and I can see those firms grabbing a lot of the market share while more traditional firms stick to what they know and bill by the hour.

I wonder how much time is spent and wasted trying to record billable time, under and over recovery and all that nonsense, when such hours could be spent so much more efficiently looking after hard-earned customers and prospects. It is mind numbing.

A simple fixed fee, fully guaranteed, has got to be the best way to sell any product or service.

How could you help to make the buying decision a much clearer and straightforward process for your client base?

POSH AND PRICELESS

A while back I was in a superstore trying to get an early morning breakfast and just after 7am I managed to find a delightful little cafe just past the main cash tills. It had a delicious array of pasties, sausage rolls, toasties, croissants, and chocolate muffins, but it was the 'posh cheese toastie' that caught my eye. I added a regular cappuccino with a sprinkling of chocolate on top, handed my cash over to the polite gentleman who took my order and sat down to enjoy the fine offering.

It wasn't until I'd polished off the delicious cheese toastie and the equally satisfying cappuccino that it occurred to me that, during my buying decision, I hadn't even noticed the price of the toastie because it had been so well presented. I couldn't even remember if there had been a price tag on it. I just admired how clever it was to glamorise a cheese toastie just by putting the word 'posh' in front of it.

Inevitably, and being an accountant, I couldn't help but take a closer look on my way out of the cafe to see exactly how visible the price was. The sumptuous display cabinet placed all the pastries below waist height and, in fact, the price on each tag was so small that it was barely visible and when I stooped to see if I could read the prices, I still

Posh and Priceless

couldn't!

I had been well and truly sold on quality alone - and a brilliant piece of marketing. It wasn't about the price. I wanted the posh cheese toastie and that was not, from my point of view, price driven. The display cabinet was wonderfully presented and was all about creating a desire for something better. If you put the effort in on that front, you can make your customers want to buy no matter what the price!
(Almost)

ANSWER THE BL**DY PHONE, WILL YOU?

When we are preparing for a Business Bootcamp, we go out of our way to systematically ring all of the attendees coming to Bootcamp to make sure they know the location, the time, and to clarify any dietary requirements.

Brace yourself for another mind-numbing rant!

It is incredible how often that, when we try to make contact by telephone (landline or mobile), the phone rings out unanswered. Often these are micro businesses whose owners are scratching their heads wondering why their business isn't growing. It beggars belief. Every missed call is a missed opportunity for the next new client or more business from an existing one. It's not only about the missed opportunity and potential financial gains that are going down the drain, I can also assure you that it's extremely irritating for your existing customers not to have their phone calls answered. So you lose on all sides.

Virtual PA services are nowhere near as expensive as they used to be and there is one firm that I believe is head and shoulders above the rest. Cost effective, very professional and, over the years I have literally sent dozens of clients to them and the feedback has always been glowing in the extreme. Call Miss Jones (www.callmissjones.co.uk) would be delighted to give you a seven-day trial of their services. It can amount to around only £40 per month plus VAT, and if you can't turn your missed calls into enough profit to cover that cost, then it sounds like you have a ticket for the Titanic and you need to change your travel plans...

All you need to do is give Call Miss Jones your email address and contact details and then let them intercept your missed calls for a week. I suggest you give them a chance to answer the telephone as they will pick it up automatically if it goes unanswered for five rings. In fact, some of my clients have been so impressed with the service they have decided to let Call Miss Jones answer all of their calls. Now, that is a recommendation!

Missed calls are missed opportunities and missed money, as well as the missed opportunity to have your calls answered professionally. They answer the phone as if you were taking the calls yourself and, as the call defaults to the service, they know that you are not available, so they will take a detailed message and contact details and email you simultaneously with the details of the call and the contact details of the caller. It's another no-brainer.

It's mind numbing not to systemise this within your business. And, by the way, I'm not on a kickback!

DEEP DOWN, ARE YOU A BUSINESS MAVERICK?

The term 'maverick' surged in popularity in 2008, propelled by the US Presidential bid of Republican Senator John McCain, who was considered a political maverick.

It hadn't taken long for the 19th century Wild West slang term for unbranded cattle that had strayed from the herd, putting their ownership in doubt, to be applied to a person who didn't follow the crowd in their thinking, and who rebelled against accepted ideas - the herd mentality.

Thus, 'maverick' came to mean an individualistic and independent thinker. In popular culture, as exemplified in the movies *Maverick* (1994) and *Top Gun* (1986), the term described colourful risk takers. Depending on context, then, 'maverick' can be applied to a pioneer who bucks current trends or to a wild and potentially reckless loose cannon.

Are you a business maverick? Do you truly 'think outside the box'? Do you refuse to play by the rules, instead preferring to take your own course of action to get results?

Start-up culture has given rise to a new brand of

thinkers: those who are no longer content to sit back and merely accept the traditional way of doing things. Mavericks are committed to getting results and aren't afraid to bend the rules to make things happen. In short, Maverick tendencies may help drive you towards success.

For mavericks, taking risks and defying convention comes with the territory. It's often second nature. Being afraid of risk is normal, but refusing to let it stop you from standing up and making a difference is the sign of a true maverick.

It's time for us to accept our maverick tendencies and harness our potential to accomplish great things. Will you be one of the mavericks who are changing the world?

IT'S ONLY KINKY THE FIRST TIME!

Don't even go there!

Call it what you like. Out of your comfort zone, being a maverick, off the beaten track, going against the grain, out of the box - let's simplify it, let's call it kinky. It only feels kinky the first time because you haven't done it before.

It means that you're not pushing your boundaries and in all likelihood, somebody else is probably already doing what you are doing. So unless you push the boundaries, whatever you are doing is not different, is not new, and it won't stop your customers and competitors in their tracks.

'Be different'. You have to stretch your imagination, and I mean really stretch it. Sitting down for a few minutes here and there to think about doing something different is not going to cut the mustard. It takes time to think deeply about how you can transform your business or find the inspiration for something that would dramatically grab the attention of your customers and prospects - an offer so compelling they'll be beating down your door.

There are businesses in your industry, no matter what it is, that are proactively trying to think

It's only kinky the first time...

dramatically outside of the box and gain that competitive advantage. If you can find that uncommon ground it will maybe put you in a position where you can charge more than just a little more for your product or service. That has to be a great place to be.

Sit down by yourself, or with your team if you have one, and think about how you can push the boundaries of your business. Think big, perhaps even to a ridiculous extent, because that will stimulate ideas and often the craziest ideas will have a grain of practicality within them.

The small guarantees, the service promises, the risk-free offers - no matter what. The more out of the ordinary your idea is, the better.

You can have a lot of fun redesigning your business, and at very little cost if you are prepared to take some risks about what you offer. Let's face it, reward never usually comes without some risk.

Think about it. It's not easy, far from it. But it sure is fun trying.

There are lots of great examples of business that do things more than a little differently.

1. There are some restaurants with no prices on the menu. You order what you want and then you pay what it was worth to you when you have finished. It sounds risky doesn't it? But it must work for them or

they wouldn't do it. It certainly gets people talking. You know the old saying, if you want people to talk about you, give them something to talk about.

2. Restaurants are great places for service examples. If you are out for a quick corporate lunch and need a super-fast turnaround, an A-board outside a restaurant telling you that 'your food order will be in front of you within 10 minutes, or your lunch is on us' will grab your attention. And takes away the worry of getting back to the office within an hour. And what fun to implement!

3. There is a hotel chain in America where you can ask any member of staff for a complete money-back refund at any time during your stay. And I mean anybody! Now there's a convincing commitment: the hotel chain is obviously well systemised and proud of the service levels it can implement day in day out, without too much risk of letting its customers down.

A SHOULDER TO LEAN ON

I have often found that business owners are perfectly capable of generating great ideas to grow their businesses, but often they don't have the guts and daring or the confidence required to see it through. Being in business can be a very lonely place sometimes, so it's good to find a coach or mentor with whom you can take a rain check and share ideas.

When I listen to new ideas arising out of my Business Development sessions, one of three things can happen. First, and best, I can say 'yes, it's a great idea'. Quite often I can see there's mileage in an idea and it's just a matter of how best to implement it as quickly and as cost effectively as possible. My experience of this scenario, however, is that doesn't happen very often.

The second thing that could happen is, I see the merit in an idea but the harsh reality is that the problems of implementing it would far outweigh the benefits, so it ends up going nowhere.

And thirdly, even worse, I listen to the idea and have to explain why it has absolutely no legs whatsoever and advise the business owner to keep their hands in their pockets and think again. From time to time this advice isn't taken and, ultimately, a lot of their time and money goes straight down the drain.

So what I'm saying is, be prepared to take that rain check. There isn't much out there that is brand new, and running your ideas past someone you trust and who knows what they are talking about could be very worthwhile.

It means you'll either have the additional confidence to press on and succeed in growing your business very quickly and profitably or, conversely, you could save yourself a fortune in unnecessary costs and sleepless nights.

So please, find a shoulder and don't be afraid to lean on it.

SLEEPWALKING

Take a long hard look at yourself in the mirror. Are you wide-awake or are you sleepwalking through your life?

I see it all the time. Business owners who get up in the morning, go to work, go through the motions, do the same things to themselves and their business day after day, week after week, for months on end - in fact, for years. They never stop and challenge themselves, never change or reinvent their business in any shape or form. They are on a relentless treadmill just doing it, doing it, doing it.

They are sleepwalking through their lives – and their business lives. Operating solely on autopilot, they don't react to changes in their environment, blind to opportunities, deaf to threats: they simply plod on, zombie-like. It's mind numbing.

Ask yourself, when was the last time you changed anything? Your website, your prices, your people, your payment terms, your strap line, your corporate logo? Let me ask you again, when was the last time you changed anything?

Too often the honest answer is 'I can't remember'. But, think about it. If you are indeed sleepwalking through your business life, that's exactly how it looks to the customers who are trying to buy from you.

There is nothing that is a more certain sign of **insanity** than to do the same thing over and over and expect **results** to be **different.**

Albert Einstein

Well, it doesn't have to be like that.

Give yourself a wake-up call and if you find you need a good slap, find somebody to slap you!

SAUSAGE MACHINE MENTALITY

I've talked a lot about thinking outside of the box. It's so difficult to do, but it's mind numbing in its simplicity when you see it done well.

I was recently in London celebrating my 20th wedding anniversary with my wife, Katie. We walked from our hotel near Kings Cross and made our way down to the river Thames near London Bridge. It was a lovely day so we thought we'd walk in the sunshine rather than taking a taxi or the underground.

I suppose over recent years I have developed a certain acuity that keeps my eyes open and looking for brilliant, but simple, ways to grow businesses of all shapes and sizes.

On our stroll, we passed a butchers' shop. Of course, the only time you visit the butchers is when you want meat, but this particular butcher had a different idea. He had set up a stall, with a hotplate thereon, immediately in front of his shop. The hotplate had a bright down lighter shining directly onto a delicious-looking, elongated sausage roll. Laid out behind were three fat jars of equally tempting sauces. From memory, I think they were a chutney and two types of mustard. The whole offer was irresistible.

The man behind the stall wore impeccable chef attire and a welcoming smile: beside him was a blackboard clearly showcasing his wares:

'Sausage roll by the inch'
'£1 per inch or £5 for 6 inches!'

I have to say it made me smile, my wife too! Needless to say, we put our hands in our pockets, pulled out a couple of quid and helped ourselves to two inches with a great big dollop of Dijon mustard. I can't begin to tell you how delicious it was.

As we parted with our cash, I couldn't help but start up a conversation with the happy chef, and I asked him how many punters, like us, were tempted throughout the day to invest in an inch or maybe even six inches of the mouth-watering sausage roll. The answer was, 'I dunno, I guess between 200 and 300 a day'.

Wow! Being an accountant, of course I did the numbers.

'So what you are saying, sir, is that you pull in an extra £200-£300 a day, at least, by putting out a little hot stove in front of your shop and selling nothing more than sausage roll, accompanied by a few sauces.' That is thinking outside the box!

Forgive me - again - for being an accountant but, annualised on a six-day week, that bright idea added an extra £1,500 a week to his takings. Assuming the take-up is always the same or even perhaps even more at certain times of the year, that's an increase in sales of over £75,000 per year. I would also think the mark-up on homemade sausage rolls would be good too so I would expect the bottom line profit before tax from this idea would be somewhere in the region of £50,000. How cool is that?

Brilliant! Simple! Extremely profitable!

What's your sausage roll? What could you do in your business without having to pull up any trees but which, by its implementation, could potentially transform your profits?

Bear in mind that this simple little butchers shop on an ordinary street, in an ordinary part of London, caused between 200 and 300 people a day to stop and buy when, under normal circumstances, they would have just passed on by the shop without a second glance.

Hardly sausage machine mentality!

BORED OR BOARD?

Here's another rant for you! This is something that makes me smile a lot.

When you drive around any city, town or village, almost everywhere you'll see large or small A-boards proudly placed in front of businesses by their owners, either on the pavement or grass verge, and aiming to entice us in with such sumptuous invitations as:

- Open for food
- Food served all day
- Fresh coffee here
- Food and coffee all day

And so on and so on...

Having put your hand deep into your pocket to pay for an A-board, at least make the most of it. Start by choosing a good quality board with some weight so that it doesn't blow over at the first breath of wind and will stand up to the elements. Then the fun can really start.

Brainstorm some ideas and come up with different messages that might just engage the passing

prospect or customer. Let's face it, it is an increasingly busy world and we spend a lot of our time sitting in traffic, making the A-board an excellent, relatively low cost opportunity to strike a chord with the passing punter.

I don't care what business you are in, there is a lot of fun to be had and if you haven't got a pavement or kerbside, then how about putting something on the outside of your business premises.

We are not just talking about restaurant and eateries, there are lots of different business it would work for:

- Top of Trip Advisor for a reason!
- Mindblowing, delicious food all day!
- A brilliant plumber is working here – call Martin on 07780...
- If your food isn't in front of you within 15 minutes, you will eat for free!

Go on, get on with it. Bored or Board?

DON'T BE STUPID!

I was reading a book a bit back, you know the type, a million and one ways to grow your business overnight. I'm afraid it was the same old crap, nothing new, no ideas that hadn't already been regurgitated time after time with a slightly different narrative and a jazzy cover. A stupid book.

And, to add insult to injury, there was an advert in the back of the book, advertising another publication about making bookkeeping easy. I can't think of anything more stupid. It even had a 30% discount bringing the price wonderfully low, in fact under £10. It was a stupid advert making a stupid suggestion that you do your own bookkeeping.

If you are bold and brave enough to run your own business, the last thing you want to be doing is your own bookkeeping. Yes, bookkeeping can be made easy, and there is some great software out there, especially Xero, which makes bookkeeping easier. But if you have any sense, you'll get out there and get selling, or work on marketing your product, rather than going home and working late into the night on your bookkeeping.

I'm sorry, but it's simply mind numbing that anyone would think that working in their business – by doing their own bookkeeping - is more valuable than working on their business.

Let the one or two decent accountants out there do your bookkeeping. It will be accurate and will stand up to investigation by HMRC.

So, don't be stupid. Trying to do your own bookkeeping is a classic example of getting your priorities wrong.

NO, REALLY, DON'T BE STUPID (PART 2)

If you do, in fact, want to be a complete and utter failure in business, here are some basic rules and guidelines, and if you follow them I can almost guarantee that you will completely and utterly cock it up!

- Make sure your website is full of grammatical errors and spelling mistakes
- Make sure the 'click here' buttons don't work or lead to an error 404 message
- Don't work on your prices. Don't test them to see whether you could pitch them higher in the market for your product or services. In fact, don't even compare them to your competitors' prices. If you know who they are.
- Don't work out which are your most profitable offerings, because if you did, you would know which ones should be promoted over than the others.
- Don't develop an attractive and effective corporate strapline or logo in case you set yourself apart from the competition. Seriously.
- Do employ someone who doesn't give a jot about customer service to take all of your calls on reception. In fact, do even better and take your time to answer the phone. It

will wind customers up immensely.

- If you have voicemail, do make sure you tell customers that their call is important to you. Then ring off before they can leave a message.
- Don't even think about having a call answering service. Obviously.
- Don't call your customers back. Or email them. Ever.

Russell Payne

YOU CAN HAVE YOUR CAKE AND EAT IT

My Business Bootcamps over the years have brought all sorts of business people into the room, owners of businesses of all shapes and sizes. There are inevitably some network marketers and, from my experience, for every two successful individuals running a network marketing team, there are another 98 who tried and failed to make anything other than a shoestring living.

There is hardly a Bootcamp that goes by without there being somebody in the room who is really only a hobbyist trying to persuade themselves that they can make a business from their passion. But, ultimately, because they only play with the idea they never really see it through to a satisfactory conclusion.

Cake-makers are a great example. They have a passion for baking and are damn good at it, but making a business out of it is a whole different affair. I met a delightful lady at a Bootcamp and she, too, had gone as far as possible to take her cake making to the next level and opened up premises in the beautiful, historic heart of Lincoln. As chance would have it, I met her following my need to buy a cake for my wife's birthday.

Once we'd sorted out my cake needs, we got to talking about the business - why wouldn't we? There was no doubt about it; this lady made delicious cakes and the spread in the shop's bay window was clear evidence of that.

'So how's it going?' I probed.

'Well, I did think we were going to run aground at one point. There were some days I took as little as £7,' she replied, with a pained expression.

Here we go again, I thought. But imagine my thoughts when she went on to say '...but we are now regularly doing around £3,000 per week and we are loving it'.

So it does show you that if you get the ingredients right, not just in the cake, but how you set out your stall - your marketing, your innovation and willingness to succeed - anything is possible, even with cakes!

So, before you give up on turning your hobby into a business, take a rain check. Seek out a business mentor and take at least one more second opinion. There are plenty of gifted people around who can advise appropriately on how to grow a business, no matter how small. Then again, as I said in an earlier chapter, if you have a ticket for the Titanic, you need to get off.

IF THIS ISN'T A WIN-WIN SCENARIO, I DON'T KNOW WHAT IS

I wish somebody would explain this to me because I just don't get it.

When you go to Spain on holiday, several of the petrol service stations have attendees ready with a smile and pump in hand to fill your car with juice, while you go off and get in the queue to pay.

Back in the UK, you get in line for the ever-increasing queues for petrol, you drag yourself out of the car, stick the nozzle in the tank and start to fill up. Very rarely do I come away without my hands splashed with petrol and, even worse, the odd drop finds it way onto my shirt cuff or trousers. At the very least I come away whiffing of the unpleasant vapour. I then join the queue with my debit card in hand cursing at being late for my next meeting. We have all been there.

So why, in Spain, do I get the delightful young lady filling up my car while I join the queue and, by the time I get to the front, the tank is full and I am ready to pay. What a great way to speed up the whole customer process.

I'm a happy customer walking back to the car, a Euro at the ready to place in the hand of the smiling recipient. What a no-brainer.

Dare I say it - I doubt my Euro finds its way into the coffers of the Spanish equivalent of the HMRC and the tax, PAYE and NIC. Even though I probably shouldn't say so, it looks like a win-win scenario to me.

Why do I go on about it? It's because I get served quicker, I get on my way quicker, and the pump attendants make a nice little cash in hand addition to their wages throughout because the throughput is that much faster.

So why can't we do this in the UK? Thoughts on a postcard, please.

Think outside of the box and think 'win-win', then everyone gets richer. Simple.

ANOTHER UPDATE ON EMPLOYMENT LAW. SERIOUSLY?

I don't care what your firm does - don't tread the same old path.

Accountants are pretty good at sticking to the safe path. You know, the annual budget breakfast, the update on employment law... yawn. In the October of 2014, we thought we would try a different type of event and we asked ourselves, how can we keep it fresh, innovative and remarkable? Defined in the dictionary as 'worthy of being noticed'.

We came up with 777 - 7 hot topics, 7 hot speakers, for 70 minutes, quarterly on the 7th.

It went down a bomb. Was it easy to find seven really good, engaging speakers every three months? No, it's difficult, but it can be done. We have had all sorts of characters and the topics we've covered have been varied, but are always interesting. Here's a sample of some of the topics we've enjoyed.

Another update on Employment Law... Seriously?

- Making resolutions stick
- Corporate branding
- Selling is a skill
- Auto Enrolment
- Facebook Pay Per Click marketing
- Cyber security risk
- The power of PR (on a budget)

I would like to think that nobody can get too bored by a 10-minute talk, and that's all they have to listen to before we move on to the next speaker and next topic. What a brilliant idea! Even if I do say so myself.

I've said it before and I'll keep on saying it – think outside the box.

And while I remember, there's been an additional, significant benefit in delivering such an event, in that almost all the speakers picked up some business from their short deliveries. Isn't it great to put on an event where everybody wins?

Why not use the 777 idea in your area - it's a no-brainer.

However, I strongly advise sticking with the 7s rather than 666. Go on, be a devil.

'OH DARLING, YOU ARE SO LAST YEAR'

When you tell people that you are a chartered accountant, you can see the shutters come down. You know they're thinking 'oh my god, I can't listen to this geezer for the next 15 minutes', and they start to look round for other people to network with.

Who can blame them? The archetypal chartered accountant – well, I'm not going there, you know what they look like and you know the stuff that drives them on. I am not saying all, just most of them.

You know the old joke 'what does a chartered accountant use as a contraceptive? Yeah, you've guessed it, his personality'. It's as old as the hills but there is some truth in it, I'm afraid.

The middle of the road accountancy practice is very good at doing what they did last year - reporting on the trading figures for the year previous to that! Let's say your trading year-end is 31st December 2014: statute dictates that we have to file those company accounts by the end of September 2015, so the work is often done in August and September 2015 - way beyond the actual trading year-end.

Oh darling, you are SO last year.

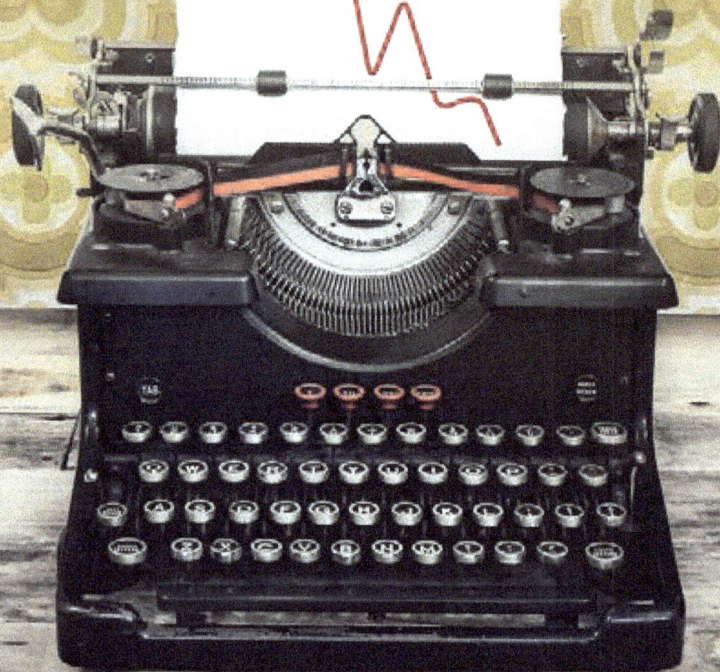

Last Year's Accounts

Summary

By the time you finally get your figures back from your 'trusted advisor' they are out of date, and all they can do is report on historical figures and tell you how much the tax bill is, or, worse, isn't.

What has dawned on me in the last five years, and even more so in the last two years, is that it should be all about next year - not last year.

Yes, we have to do the sausage machine stuff and report on last year's accounts, but the real value to bring to the table is information that helps the business owner move forward, set plans, set growth targets and ultimately build a better business, and beyond that, a better life. Hallelujah!

If you are in business, ask yourself 'what exactly do we get from our accountant'. If the answer is 'last year', then you are not getting everything you need. Ask for more. Get more!

It's all about next year. We can't change last year; we can only report on it. What a bundle of laughs that is.

This book is pregnant with ideas that are currently leading edge, and my overriding advice to you as a business owner is to be an early adopter of everything that is innovative and different.

So go and find yourself an accountant who is switched on and who can take you through the next couple of years and beyond, rather than simply reporting on the last decade as they probably have done!

'Oh darling, you are so next year'.

YOU NEED TO GET OFF!

A while back, at one of our Business Bootcamps, I met a woman who had been running an online business directory in a small rural town for about two years. During the Bootcamp, I began talking about building businesses using all the latest tools and resources, and I could see her glaze over somewhat as she drifted into another place. I don't know where it was, but it was definitely a long way from where we were.

It wasn't until I read her feedback form after the event that I realised that what I'd seen was a penny in the process of dropping.

We only really get this one life to make a difference, to make a living, to build a sustainable business and, at the end of it, something we can sell or take a pension income from forever and ever. If the business isn't doing that for you, then it's not a real business.

Clearly this lady had got to thinking, and her feedback did, in fact, mention that she had been doing some 'soul searching'. As a direct result of Bootcamp she had decided to do a complete U-turn and go back to her former specialism in procurement and supply chain consultancy. She'd realised she

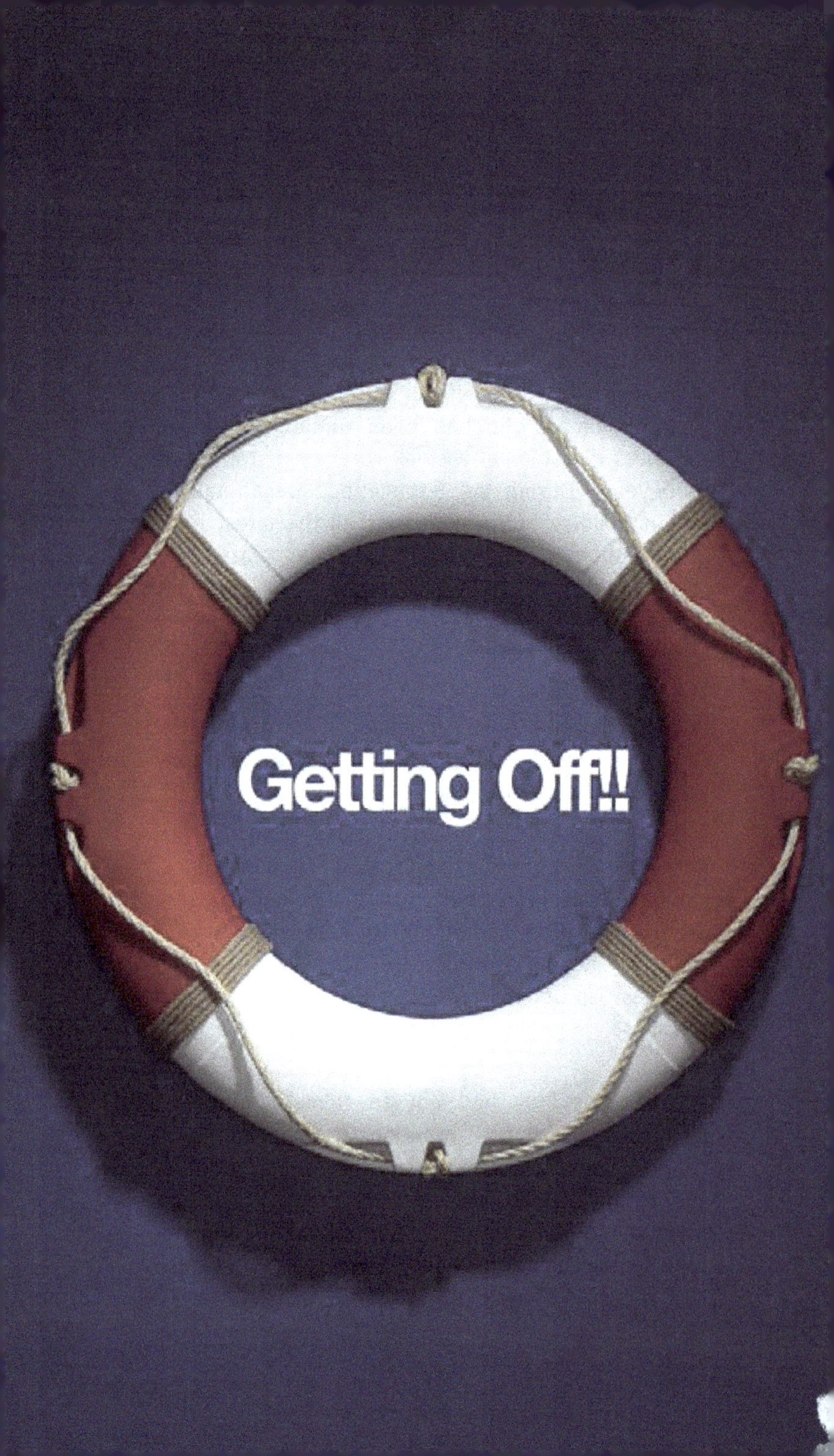
Getting Off!!

wasn't running a sustainable business and decided there and then to make a change for the better.

Sometimes the business journey is not always a smooth or pleasant experience for business owners, but when the evidence is right in front of you, it's wise to pay attention to it and take some action. If you are sitting on the fence, get off on one side or the other. If you choose the wrong side it doesn't matter, you can always get to the other side. But sitting on the fence and doing nothing is strictly for numpties.

If you have a ticket for the Titanic, you need to get off!!

NO EXCUSES FOR NOT KNOWING, PLEASE!

If you are a business owner spending a boatload of cash on marketing, there is no excuse for not knowing what your return on investment is, no matter what platform you are using for advertising purposes.

We've talked about PPC at length, and that is very easy to monitor along with Google Analytics, so no excuse there.

If you have a system for recording where every new piece of business comes from, either through conversation or website pixels, again, there is no excuse on that front.

If you are doing a lot of paper advertising, i.e. in local magazines and newspapers, together with a hotchpotch of online marketing and visits to your website, there is an easy way of gauging where all your leads come from. So, if you are going to invest a big chunk of your hard earned money into a multifaceted marketing campaign, I suggest you take note of this.

Telephone tracking numbers are a low-cost, easy to implement way of monitoring response rates, and this is how they work.

You buy a handful of different telephone numbers that ultimately all go through to your main landline number. So, for example, if you have an advert on the radio, you would use a unique telephone number for that purpose and repeat, with different tracking numbers for all the other individual campaigns - on your website, newspaper advertising, church magazine or whatever. You can then dip into the reports and see exactly who responded and when they rang each number and compare that to the converted sales with the initial outlay of each campaign.

A simple system to monitor which campaigns achieve which results. So don't ever say that you are doing a lot of marketing but you don't know which form is the most effective!

Tracking telephone numbers: easy to implement, simple to manage and very cost effective.

Get on track!

AND FINALLY...

I am going to leave you with a short checklist of my Top Ten Picks – in no particular order – of the things you really should address in building your world-class business.

1. DDWT
2. An A-Board not an A Bored
3. Use it or lose it
4. Say yes to corporate video
5. Paper Click Marketing
6. 1%, 2%, 5% or 20%
7. About Us
8. Sausage machine mentality
9. Same old, same old
10. DDWT (yes – again!)

Good luck. These will make a difference – a big one.

Acknowledgements

David Gill – for planting the seed that grew into Business Bootcamp and for being a true friend

Peter Thomson – for DDWT. Peter I don't know whether it's yours, but here's the credit anyway

Wallbreaker.co.uk – You guys are awesome, what a journey

Russell Payne & Co Ltd – the Team, these people have given me the platform to make everything possible, even time to write a book!

Stella – our office dog. The ultimate warm welcome.

Janet Marshall – for all the copywriting, and the early morning coffees.

Geoff Ramm – the tipping point for making me write this book

Taryn Johnston - Finishing it all off, its been fun

Katie Susan Payne – well what can I say?

www.ingramcontent.com/pod-product-compliance
Lightning Source LLC
Chambersburg PA
CBHW060444240326
41598CB00087B/3418